DEMOL

EVIL

FOUNDATIONS

Moses Nsubuga Sekatawa

DEMOLISHING EVIL FOUNDATIONS

Moses Nsubuga Sekatawa

Copyright © 2016 by Moses Nsubuga Sekatawa

ISBN-10: **9970-883-06-2** (Uganda Publishers Ass'n)

Copyright © 2016 by Moses Nsubuga Sekatawa

ISBN-13: **978-1500426750**

ISBN-10: **150042675X**

United States of America

Moses Nsubuga Sekatawa

Dedication

To my dear daughter Rachael.

There are millions out there desperate for a permanent solution to the invisible challenges that have limited their families and bloodlines for generations.

You obviously have a good foundation in Christ. According to Jeremiah 1:9-10, the Lord has put His words in your mouth and set you "over the nations and over the kingdoms, to root out, and to pull down, and to destroy, and to throw down, to build, and to plant".

So arise, stand strong and continue being a blessing to as many as the Lord will enable you to reach in the mighty Name of our Lord Jesus Christ, the Son of the Living God.

Scriptural quotations are all derived from the Authorized (King James) Version of the Bible unless otherwise specified.

Sometimes they have been interpreted or simply alluded to, to suit individual application. Translations and paraphrases are all by me.

Needless to say, the nouns and pronouns by which satan and his cohorts are addressed do not bear any capital letters in this book unless it is a printing error.

Yours in Christ,

Moses Nsubuga Sekatawa.

Contents

Chapter

1.

Foundations.

A foundation is the basis upon which a thing stands and is supported. Foundations are normally laid with a provision for future maintenance and improvement.

Every establishment has a foundation. Some houses are built upon a strong foundation. Such are the houses which stand in the midst of so many challenges. Some houses are built upon a weak foundation. Others would have stood but there was a crack in their foundation. What a painful day when an engineer tells you to demolish your skyscraper just because there is a crack in its foundation which you might have taken for granted! So it is with our lives. Our Lord Jesus said:

24. Therefore whosoever heareth these sayings of Mine, and doeth them, I will liken him unto a wise man, which built his house upon a rock:

25. And the rain descended, and the floods came, and the winds blew, and beat upon that house; and it fell not: for it was founded upon a rock.

26. And every one that heareth these sayings of Mine, and doeth them not, shall be likened unto a

foolish man, which built his house upon the sand:

27.   And the rain descended, and the floods came, and the winds blew, and beat upon that house; and it fell: and great was the fall of it.

- Matthew 7:24-27.

It is not uncommon to see magnificent structures established upon weak and shaky foundations.   Just like we see buildings in the material world, some things can be built in the realm of the unseen.   The strength of any building depends so much on the foundation upon which it stands.

We talk about buildings, systems, nations and so much more because people exist and not otherwise.   The greatest person you ever saw was once a baby. The greatest family you ever saw was once a man and his wife. The greatest empire you ever saw or heard about was once an idea carried by one person.

That great family or nation has a foundation. It has ideals and values by which stands. The ideals and values of that family or nation form its culture which finally becomes a reflection of who their influence is.

Our lives need to be founded upon the Word of God. Other foundations may seem beautiful but the only sure and eternally firm foundation is the Word of God.

> 11. For other foundation can no man lay than that is laid, which is Jesus Christ.
>
> - 1 Corinthians 3:11.

In this book we will fix our attention on personal and family foundations.

Chapter

2.

Strong men, shaky foundations

The Bible is not silent about God's great servants whose shaky foundations failed to support weight of their charisma. The things we read about concerning the servants of God in the Bible were written for admonition.

11. Now all these things happened unto them for ensamples: and they are written for

our admonition, upon whom the ends of the world are come.

- 1 Corinthians 10:11.

We will look at Jacob, Moses and Elijah so as to get a clearer picture of what shaky foundations can do in the life of a person.

1.   God's covenant friend Jacob

24.   And Jacob was left alone; and there wrestled a man with him until the breaking of the day.

25.   And when He saw that he prevailed not against him, He touched the hollow of his thigh; and the hollow of Jacob's thigh

was out of joint, as He wrestled with him.

26. And He said, Let me go, for the day breaketh. And he said, I will not let thee go, except thou bless me.

27. And He said unto him, What *is* thy name? And he said, Jacob.

28. And He said, Thy name shall be called no more Jacob, but Israel: for as a prince hast thou power with God and with men, and hast prevailed.

29. And Jacob asked *Him*, and said, Tell *me*, I pray Thee, Thy Name. And He said,

Wherefore *is* it *that* thou dost ask after My Name? And he blessed him there.

30. And Jacob called the name of the place Peniel: for I have seen God face to face, and my life is preserved.

- Genesis 32:24-30.

That was the turning point in Jacob's life. God gave him a new name symbolizing a new beginning. No longer was he to be called Jacob (supplanter, trickster). His new name became ISRA-EL. He was a prince ordained by God. The crack in his family foundation was dealt with. It takes an encounter with God to deal with the cracks in one's foundation.

Where was the crack in Jacob's foundation? I am glad you asked. The closet people in

Jacob's paternal ancestry were Abraham and Isaac. The closest people in his maternal ancestry were Sarah and Rebecca the sister of Laban.

Abraham lied about his wife in the presence of a king saying she was not a wife to him.[1] Isaac his son was no better. He too lied about his wife saying she was a sister to him.[2] Jacob's grandmother, Sarah was no better either. She consented to Abraham's lie about his relationship with her surrendering herself to the discretion of Abimelech king of Gerar.[3]

Rebekkah was worse. She connived with Jacob her younger son to rob Esau of a blessing from his father even at the risk of a curse.[4] Her brother Laban was a trickster. He

---

[1] Genesis 20:2.

[2] Genesis 26:6-11.

[3] Genesis 20:5

[4] Genesis 27:1-29.

gave a wrong bride to Jacob after making him work for seven years.[5] Then he played so many tricks to try and rob Jacob of his wages.[6]

Such was the ancestry of Jacob, God's covenant friend. They might have had so many good things but integrity was hardly one of them.

Jacob's name meant a supplanter.[7] His turning point came when he walked away from his uncle and wrestled with God. His identity was changed. He got a new name, Israel.[8]

2.   Moses the Levite.

Jacob settled in Shalem, a city of Shechem.[9]

---

[5] Genesis 29:15-30.

[6] Genesis 30:25-43.

[7] Genesis 27:36.

[8] Genesis 32:28.

[9] Genesis 33:18

His daughter Dinah went out to se the daughters of the land. A prince of the country saw her, *"took her, and lay with her, and defiled her"*.[10] This was a disgrace to the family of Jacob the new immigrant.

Later on the young man's father, Hamor approached Jacob asking for his son to be allowed to marry Dinah. The sons of Jacob deceived him that all would be well if he only allowed all his men to be circumcised. All the men of the land consented to the *'deal'* and allowed themselves to be circumcised. There was more to be expected from this covenant. Unknown to all the men of the city was the fact that this *'deal'* was a key to their destruction.

20. And Hamor and Shechem his son came unto the gate of their city, and communed with the men of their city, saying,

---

[10] Genesis 34:2.

21. These men *are* peaceable with us; therefore let them dwell in the land, and trade therein; for the land, behold, *it is* large enough for them; let us take their daughters to us for wives, and let us give them our daughters.

22. Only herein will the men consent unto us for to dwell with us, to be one people, if every male among us be circumcised, as they *are* circumcised.

23. *Shall* not their cattle and their substance and every beast of theirs *be* ours? only let us consent unto them, and they will dwell with us.

24. And unto Hamor and unto Shechem his son hearkened all

that went out of the gate of his city; and every male was circumcised, all that went out of the gate of his city.

25.   And it came to pass on the third day, when they were sore, that two of the sons of Jacob, Simeon and Levi, Dinah's brethren, took each man his sword, and came upon the city boldly, and slew all the males.

26.   And they slew Hamor and Shechem his son with the edge of the sword, and took Dinah out of Shechem's house, and went out.

27.   The sons of Jacob came upon the slain, and spoiled the city, because they had defiled their sister.

28.   They took their sheep, and their oxen, and their asses, and that which *was* in the city, and that which *was* in the field,

29.   and all their wealth, and all their little ones, and their wives took they captive, and spoiled even all that *was* in the house.

- Genesis 34:20-29.

What a tragedy that was to the city! After all was said and done Jacob was so troubled. He feared for his life and for the lives of his loved ones with him. His people were few in number compared to the inhabitants of the land.[11] In case of any retaliation, he didn't seem to have enough power to keep the enemy at bay.

---

[11] Genesis 34:30-31.

Later on Jacob spoke to all his sons before he died. He had no kind words for the anger of Simeon and Levi. He cursed their fierce anger and their cruel wrath.

5. Simeon and Levi *are* brethren; instruments of cruelty *are in* their habitations.

6. O my soul, come not thou into their secret; unto their assembly, mine honour, be not thou united: for in their anger they slew a man, and in their selfwill they digged down a wall.

7. Cursed *be* their anger, for *it was* fierce; and their wrath, for it was cruel: I will divide them in Jacob, and scatter them in Israel.

- Genesis 49:5-7.

After that we have a very interesting occurrence. A male descendant of Levi got married to a female descendant of Levi. That was the bloodline from which Moses, the servant of God came.[12]

a.   He slew the Egyptian

The first record we have of Moses after he grows up is of him slaying an Egyptian. He could hardly contain his anger when he saw a Hebrew being smitten by the Egyptian.

> 11.   And it came to pass in those days, when Moses was grown, that he went out unto his brethren, and looked on their burdens: and he spied an Egyptian smiting an Hebrew, one of his brethren.

---

[12] Exodus 2:1-11.

12.   And he looked this way and that way, and when he saw that *there was* no man, he slew the Egyptian, and hid him in the sand.

- Exodus 2:11-12.

Moses had to flee and leave the comfort of the palace because Pharaoh got to know about it. What a painful day that was for a man raised as a prince in the greatest known civilization of his time to end up in a wilderness just because of his anger!

When Moses got to Midian after fleeing from the wrath of Pharaoh, he started with a fight. Yes, the motive was good but it was a fight.[13] Daughters to Jethro, the priest of Midian needed help because of the shepherds who always troubled them at the well.   Moses finally settled in the land of Midian.   One of those girls, Zipporah was given to him for a wife by her father.

---

[13] Exodus 2:15-19.

b. He broke the Ten Commandments

So many years later, God appeared to Moses in a burning bush and gave him a divine assignment to deliver the Israel from the Egyptian bondage. We are told Moses *"the man Moses was very meek, above all the men which were upon the face of the earth"*.[14] It is ironic that this very meek man had some great outbursts anger which sometimes affected his life and ministry.

We see Moses' anger after God gave him the two tablets on which the ten commandments were written. Moses descended from the Mountain to go to the camp of the children of Israel. When he got to the camp, he realized there was sin in the camp.

> 15.   And Moses turned, and went down from the mount, and the two tables of the testimony *were* in his

---

[14] Numbers 12:3.

hand: the tables *were* written on both their sides; on the one side and on the other *were* they written.

16.   And the tables *were* the work of God, and the writing *was* the writing of God, graven upon the tables.

17.   And when Joshua heard the noise of the people as they shouted, he said unto Moses, *There is* a noise of war in the camp.

18.   And he said, *It is* not the voice of *them that* shout for mastery, neither *is it* the voice of *them* that cry for being overcome: but the noise of them that sing do I hear.

- Exodus 32:15-18.

That was absurd. They were worshipping an idol instead of the covenant keeping God who delivered them from slavery. How could a people who saw great miracles and wonders end up worshipping an idol? Did Aaron have to be part of this stupidity? Moses couldn't take it. His *"anger waxed hot"*.[15]

> 19.   And it came to pass, as soon as he came nigh unto the camp, that he saw the calf, and the dancing: and Moses' anger waxed hot, and he cast the tables out of his hands, and brake them beneath the mount.
>
> - Exodus 32:19.

The Bible says *"all have sinned and fallen short of the glory of God"*.[16] We have all broken God's laws almost every moment of our lives. Sometimes we break two or three

---

[15] Exodus 32:19

[16] Romans 3:23.

laws. I have had some people make fun of Moses saying he was the greatest sinner because he broke all the Ten Commandments at once.

> 20. And he took the calf which they had made, and burnt *it* in the fire, and ground *it* to powder, and strawed *it* upon the water, and made the children of Israel drink *of it*.

> 21. And Moses said unto Aaron, What did this people unto thee, that thou hast brought so great a sin upon them?

> 22. And Aaron said, Let not the anger of my lord wax hot: thou knowest the people, that they *are set* on mischief.

> - Exodus 32:15-22.

In a world where there was no electricity or gas, it obviously took a lot of time for Moses to burn a calf in fire, grind it to powder and straw it upon water and force everyone to drink of it. We have no idea of how many hours Moses spent under the influence of this anger. What could his face have appeared like for that multitude to obey his command? The meekest man on the planet was raging. Even Aaron; his big brother was so scared of him.

c.   He smote the Rock

Many times, God bears with us and continues to use us for His glory not because we are perfect but because of His mercy and grace. *"The LORD is longsuffering, and of great mercy"*.[17]   Sometimes servants of God misconstrue the presence of miracles in their ministries to betoken acceptability by God. Moses did not learn to control his anger. He continued to serve God without dealing with this problem inherited from his ancestry.

---

[17] Numbers 14:18.

1.   Then came the children of Israel, *even* the whole congregation, into the desert of Zin in the first month: and the people abode in Kadesh; and Miriam died there, and was buried there.

2.   And there was no water for the congregation: and they gathered themselves together against Moses and against Aaron.

3.   And the people chode with Moses, and spake, saying, Would God that we had died when our brethren died before the LORD!

4.   And why have ye brought up the congregation of the LORD into this wilderness, that we and our cattle should die there?

5.   And wherefore have ye made us to come up out of Egypt, to bring us in unto this evil place? it *is* no place of seed, or of figs, or of vines, or of pomegranates; neither *is* there any water to drink.

6.   And Moses and Aaron went from the presence of the assembly unto the door of the tabernacle of the congregation, and they fell upon their faces: and the glory of the LORD appeared unto them.

7.   And the LORD spake unto Moses, saying,

8.   Take the rod, and gather thou the assembly together, thou, and Aaron thy brother, and speak ye unto the rock before their eyes; and it shall give forth his water,

and thou shalt bring forth to them water out of the rock: so thou shalt give the congregation and their beasts drink.

9.   And Moses took the rod from before the LORD, as He commanded him.

10. And Moses and Aaron gathered the congregation together before the rock, and he said unto them, Hear now, ye rebels; must we fetch you water out of this rock?

11. And Moses lifted up his hand, and with his rod he smote the rock twice: and the water came out abundantly, and the congregation drank, and their beasts *also*.

12.   And the LORD spake unto Moses and Aaron, Because ye believed Me not, to sanctify Me in the eyes of the children of Israel, therefore ye shall not bring this congregation into the land which I have given them.

13.   This *is* the water of Meribah; because the children of Israel strove with the LORD, and He was sanctified in them.

- Numbers 20:1-13.

In the seventh and eighth verse of the scripture we have just read, God told Moses to speak to the rock before the children of Israel. That was all Moses needed to do in order for the congregation and their beasts to have water. It appears Moses was too angry to listen to God. Anger always causes us to miss out on the necessary details in life. He *"took the rod from before the LORD, as He commanded him"*[18] and he smote the rock twice! Later on we are told the Spiritual Rock that followed them was Christ.[19] So Moses smote Christ twice.

The tenth verse reveals so much pride and arrogance in Moses' words before he smites the Rock.

> 10. And Moses and Aaron gathered the congregation together before the rock, and he said unto them, Hear now, ye rebels; must we fetch you water out of this rock?
>
> - Numbers 20:10.

He behaved as though God's power was limited without him. He sounded like God and

---

[18] Numbers 20:9.

[19] 1 Corinthians 10:4.

him and God were two divine beings working miracles together. *"Hear now, ye rebels; must we fetch you water out of this rock?"* – Numbers 20:10.

Beloved, God has by His grace chosen to work with and through us to bless His people. However, we should not be blinded to the fact that He is sovereign and can do everything without us. For example, did He need our intercession in order to raise up Jesus from the dead? Or does He need our intercession in order to uphold all things by the Word of His power?[20] He is God, and we are not. The earlier we accept this, the better it will be for us in our lives and ministries.

I have heard a man of God saying, "We work miracles" because one of the gifts of the Holy Spirit is the working of miracles – 1 Corinthians 12:10. It is important to note that that is not a man's gift; it is the gift of the Holy

---

[20] Hebrews 1:3.

Spirit. The gifts of the Holy Spirit operate at His discretion; not yours.[21] God is not obliged to give you any credit for the gifts of the Holy Spirit. The Holy Spirit is not a creature to be manipulated. He is God.[22]

Yes, God gave them water. Was He pleased with Moses? Evidently NO. Moses had taken God for granted and abused His grace for so long. There were miracles, signs and wonders in his ministry not because he was a good man but because God loved His people. This time he took the joke to far. God was not amused.

One of the scaring truths about God is that He is Supreme. He is immutable. His decisions are unchangeable. By this act of disobedience, God said Moses should not enter the Promised Land and so it was. Moses' anger had finally affected his destiny.

---

[21] 1 Corinthians 12:11.

[22] Acts 5:3-4; 1 Corinthians 3:16-17; Philippians 2:13.

Where was this problem from? It was from his ancestry. He went into ministry without dealing with it. It affected his relationship with God. It affected his ministry partners. It affected his own life. His shaky foundation could not support the magnificence of his glorious ministry.

3. Elijah the prophet of fire:

Elijah was a great servant of God. His ministry was characterized with so many amazing wonders. The drought was in his mouth, so were the rains.[23] He raised the dead and so much more.[24] One time after a great revival, Jezebel threatened him with death. Elijah fled for his life and said something to the effect that there was an evil trend in his family which his life identified with.

---

[23] 1 Kings 17:1.

[24] 1 Kings 17:17-23.

1.   And Ahab told Jezebel all that Elijah had done, and withal how he had slain all the prophets with the sword.

2.   Then Jezebel sent a messenger unto Elijah, saying, So let the gods do *to me*, and more also, if I make not thy life as the life of one of them by to morrow about this time.

3.   And when he saw *that*, he arose, and went for his life, and came to Beer-sheba, which *belongeth* to Judah, and left his servant there.

4.   he himself went a day's journey into the wilderness, and came and sat down under a juniper tree: and he requested for himself that he might die; and said, It is enough; now, O LORD,

take away my life; for I *am* not
better than my fathers.

- 1 Kings 19:1-4.

Elijah was not better that his fathers. What
could the problem have been? Did all his
male ancestors die at that age? Was there a
monster of trauma which always attacked
anyone that seemed prosperous in his
bloodline? What was it in his life that was so
traumatic yet not strange to his ancestors?
We are not told specifically what it was. All
we know is that he was struggling with
something his ancestors failed to conquer. It
was at his foundation.

The list of God's generals who struggled with
weak foundations is so long. We could talk
about Jeremiah's exasperation when he cried
out in Lamentations 5:7, *"Our fathers have
sinned, and are not; and we have borne their
iniquities"*. We could bring it to our day and
observe our very own lives. The key lies in

identifying the problem and dealing with it from a scriptural perspective.

Chapter

3

Hezekiah
the selfish parent

It is easy to be deceived that all parents are so loving and would lay their lives down for the sake of their children. This is not always true. Some parents compete with their children. Others strive to succeed at the expense of their children's future. They are so determined to have their way regardless of what it may cost the next generation. It is also true that some leaders plunge their nations into great trouble because all they think about is themselves. They live, speak and make decisions as if life is all about them alone. It is so painful when selfishness reigns in the heart of a leader.

Hezekiah was a man who loved and served God yet his love for his children was not complete. As long as he stayed out of trouble, he did not mind what pain his children had to put up with.

1.   In those days was Hezekiah sick unto death. And the prophet Isaiah the son of Amoz came to him, and said unto him, Thus saith the LORD, Set thine house in order; for thou shalt die, and not live.

2.   Then he turned his face to the wall, and prayed unto the LORD, saying,

3. I beseech thee, O LORD, remember now how I have walked before thee in truth and with a perfect heart, and have done *that which is* good in thy sight. And Hezekiah wept sore.

4. And it came to pass, afore Isaiah was gone out into the middle court, that the word of the LORD came to him, saying,

5. Turn again, and tell Hezekiah the captain of my people, Thus saith the LORD, the God of David thy father, I have heard thy prayer, I have seen thy tears: behold, I will heal thee: on the third day thou shalt go up unto the house of the LORD.

6.　And I will add unto thy days fifteen years; and I will deliver thee and this city out of the hand of the king of Assyria; and I will defend this city for Mine own sake, and for My servant David's sake.

7.　And Isaiah said, Take a lump of figs. And they took and laid *it* on the boil, and he recovered.

8.　And Hezekiah said unto Isaiah, What *shall be* the sign that the LORD will heal me, and that I shall go up into the house of the LORD the third day?

9.　And Isaiah said, This sign shalt thou have of the LORD, that the LORD will do the thing that He hath spoken: shall the shadow go forward ten degrees, or go back ten degrees?

10. And Hezekiah answered, It is a light thing for the shadow to go down ten degrees: nay, but let the shadow return backward ten degrees.

11. And Isaiah the prophet cried unto the LORD: and He brought the shadow ten degrees backward, by which it had gone down in the dial of Ahaz.

12. At that time Berodach-baladan, the son of Baladan, king of Babylon, sent letters and a present unto Hezekiah: for he had heard that Hezekiah had been sick.

13. And Hezekiah hearkened unto them, and shewed them all the house of his precious things, the silver, and the gold, and the spices, and the precious ointment, and *all* the house of his armour, and all that was found in his treasures: there was nothing in his house, nor in all his dominion, that Hezekiah shewed them not.

14. Then came Isaiah the prophet unto king Hezekiah, and said unto him, What said these men? and from whence came they unto thee? And Hezekiah said, They are come from a far country, *even* from Babylon.

15. And he said, What have they seen in thine house? And Hezekiah answered, All *the things* that *are* in mine house have they seen: there is nothing among my

treasures that I have not shewed them.

16. And Isaiah said unto Hezekiah, Hear the word of the LORD.

17. Behold, the days come, that all that *is* in thine house, and that which thy fathers have laid up in store unto this day, shall be carried into Babylon: nothing shall be left, saith the LORD.

18. And of thy sons that shall issue from thee, which thou shalt beget, shall they take away; and they shall be eunuchs in the palace of the king of Babylon.

19. Then said Hezekiah unto Isaiah, Good *is* the word of the LORD which thou hast spoken. And he said, *Is it* not *good*, if peace and truth be in my days?

- 2 Kings 20:1-19.

When Hezekiah was ill, he cried desperately to the Lord for his healing. It was not because he was concerned about his children's plight in case he died. He was simply concerned about himself. Not even about his subjects as a king. He did not mention anyone else in his prayer. It was all about himself.

After Hezekiah was healed, he initiated trouble by showing all the treasures of his kingdom to the Babylonians. Unknown to him was the danger that would result from this foolish mistake. All that he displayed would be taken to Babylon. His children would become eunuchs which meant no continuity of his bloodline. He had foolishly played into the hands of his enemies.

One would expect a king to cry out to the Lord for mercy so that this judgment is averted. That was not the case with King Hezekiah. He rejoiced because the trouble for his sins was not to be endured by him but by his children. It grieves my heart to read the nineteenth verse; *"Then said Hezekiah unto Isaiah, Good is the word of the LORD which thou hast spoken. And he said, Is it not good, if peace and truth be in my days?"*

What a parent! He did not mind what the next generation had to put up with as long as he had a good time.

As a result of my deliverance ministry, I have been privileged to interact with so many people in my life. It hurts to learn the things that hold some of them in bondage.

I have met some people whose misery began when their parents went to a witch and dedicated the whole family to satan in exchange for fame and fortune. I remember one case which I dealt with where poverty and premature death reigned over a family. In this family every male child died at the age of twenty-nine. No one lived to see his thirtieth birthday.

This young man came to our Church for a prayer of deliverance. He was so gripped with fear and frustration as he narrated the underlying ordeal which served as a foundation for his misery.

They were very poor as a family. The parents could not afford to pay tuition for them. It was always a struggle for the family to have food and clothing. Whoever wanted a definition of poverty simply had to look at this family.

Weary with the status quo, both parents agreed to consult a satanic priest. They were initiated into a covenant so as to have the wealth they desired. Covenants have four major pillars:

    a. Terms and conditions.
    b. Promises and warnings.
    c. Responsibilities.
    d. Seals. tokens and symbols.

Therefore terms and conditions were spelt out which they had to meet. Promises and warnings were pronounced depending on how faithful or unfaithful they would be to the covenant. Responsibilities were assigned to them as part of the requirements of this covenant to remain valid. Tokens were exchanged to ratify and seal the covenant.

What were the terms and conditions?

The parents had to sacrifice their first born son at a satanic altar. They had to pledge allegiance to the powers of darkness and to the satanic priest. They made oaths to the effect that as long as they were granted wealth, demons had a right a right to *'oversee the family and be part of it'.*

What were the promises and warnings?

In exchange to their sacrifice and oaths of allegiance, the parents were promised wealth, a great social status and fame. They were also warned never to violate the covenant terms by doing or saying anything which would compromise their allegiance to satan. If they ever did, their lives would be in danger.

What were the responsibilities?

Every year they had to slaughter bulls and renew their allegiance to the powers of darkness at the direction of the satanic priest.

What were the tokens?

The tokens were some fetishes they could wear under their garments and a few marks tattooed on their bodies. These tokens were the seals of the covenant and the sign that this family was in a covenant relationship with the powers of darkness.

It is true that this family got riches and became very famous. Their status changed for some time. The pleasures of sin have a very limited shelf life Their season always comes to an end.[1] A few years after they got the riches, their season of sinful pleasures ended. Both parents died mysteriously.

Their death did not stop the powers of darkness from perpetuating their diabolic agenda against the family. They had been invited and given legal right by the parents. They were in a covenant relationship with the family.

I led this young man in a prayer of repentance. That evil covenant was

---

[1] Hebrews 11:25.

renounced and broken. After that I ministered deliverance to him and he was set free by the power of God. Seventeen years after that he is still alive and well. For more information about covenants please read my book, *"Break the curses".*

There are so many people struggling today because of words spoken by their parents before they were born or as they grew up. A parent wields so much authority and it should be used to bless and never to curse his children or limit their progress in any way.

There is good news for those who struggle because their biological or adoptive parents spoke curses over their lives. The good news is that there is a Father in heaven Who is by far so much superior to any earthly fathers. His Name is Almighty God. He has given us His Word (Bible) and called us to be beneficiaries of the covenant by the blood of His Son Jesus Christ. It does not matter what curses were ever laid upon your life. Those curses can and should be broken in the Name of Jesus. You are entitled to your freedom.

.

Chapter

4.

Childhood problems

The early stages of every person's life are the most delicate and vulnerable ones. It is at this stage that children are given a strong foundation and others are surrendered to the attacks of the enemy. We are instructed to *"train up a child in the way he should go: and when he is old, he will not depart from it."* – Proverbs 22:6.

Children born into God fearing families where the Word of God and prayer are emphasized receive a better foundation than those born outside such a provision. Children born into families where works of the flesh flourish[1] are more prone to curses and demonic bondages.[2]

A very sad biblical story is given us of a father whose son was tormented by a dumb spirit since his childhood. It always strangled him causing him to foam, gnash his teeth and pine away. It knew where the water was. It knew where the fire was. It kept a program. It was intelligent. The disciples of Jesus laboured against it for so long without any success. It defied their commands. Then the Lord Jesus came on the scene. It recognized the authority of Jesus. Everything changed.

> 14. And when He came to His disciples, He saw a great

---

[1] Galatians 5:19-21.

[2] Proverbs 3:33, Lamentations 5:7-13.

multitude about them, and the scribes questioning with them.

15. And straightway all the people, when they beheld Him, were greatly amazed, and running to Him saluted Him.

16. And He asked the scribes, What question ye with them?

17. And one of the multitude answered and said, Master, I have brought unto Thee my son, which hath a dumb spirit;

18. And wheresoever he taketh him, he teareth him: and he foameth, and gnasheth with his teeth, and pineth away: and I spake to thy disciples that they

should cast him out; and they could not.

19. He answereth him, and saith, O faithless generation, how long shall I be with you? how long shall I suffer you? bring him unto Me.

20. And they brought him unto Him: and when he saw Him, straightway the spirit tare him; and he fell on the ground, and wallowed foaming.

21. And He asked his father, How long is it ago since this came unto him? And he said, Of a child.

22. And ofttimes it hath cast him into the fire, and into the waters, to

destroy him: but if Thou canst do any thing, have compassion on us, and help us.

23.   Jesus said unto him, If thou canst believe, all things are possible to him that believeth.

24.   And straightway the father of the child cried out, and said with tears, Lord, I believe; help thou mine unbelief.

- Mark 9:14-24.

Whenever the Lord asks a question, He is not looking for information. It is always for our sake that He asks. In the Old Testament we find occasions when God asked questions. For example He asked Adam, "Where art thou?"[3] He asked Cain, "Where is Abel, thy

---

[3] Genesis 3:9.

brother?"[4]   In the New Testament the Lord Jesus asked Saul of Tarsus, "Saul, Saul, why persecutes thou Me?"[5]   I am so glad the Lord Jesus asked the boy's father a question.   It was for all of us.

> 21.   And He asked his father, How long is it ago since this came unto him? And he said, Of a child.
>
> - Mark 9:21.

More than likely, this boy was born without a demonic problem. He must have lived a good life until something happened to him which rendered him susceptible demonic oppression. We are not given any details about the source of the problem. All we know is that there was a time when he was vulnerable and a demon took advantage of it to oppress him.

---

[4] Genesis 4:9.

[5] Acts 8:4.

People are most vulnerable when young. I have met many people whose problems began during their early childhood years. It is the responsibility of parents to always do their best to ensure the safety of their children. For example children have always been cautioned; *"Stranger, danger"* for fear of the potential dangers posed by unknown people. There is a painful story of Jacob's daughter, Dinah who wondered around after they settled in a new city and she was sexually abused by a prince of that region.[6] It is at such moments that a door of someone's life is opened to sorrow and demonic oppression.

1. Traumatized when young.

A young woman came to our Church in Kampala, Uganda. She loved the Lord but was oppressed by demons. A spirit husband always raped her during the nights. She would become paralyzed and unable to defend herself whenever it attacked her.

---

[6] Genesis 34:1-2.

How did this ordeal begin? I am glad you asked. Konge (not her real name) was born to unmarried teenage parents. They were not committed to each other and they were not prepared for the challenges that come with a baby. The parents of her teenage mother rejected Baby Konge during her infancy. As far as they were concerned, she belonged to another family and was never meant to be their responsibility. They regarded the baby a disgrace to their family's reputation. Therefore, the young man took her to his parents' home.

The culture of Konge's people just like many other cultures has some loopholes that can easily be exploited by the powers of darkness. In that culture, a grandfather jokingly calls his granddaughters, wives. A grandmother calls her grandsons, husbands. Your sister in law is jokingly called your wife. A woman's brother in law is jokingly regarded as her husband. Such careless statements easily open the door to spirits of promiscuity. It is against that background that Konge's early childhood was formed. She, supposedly grew up in the home of her '*husband*'.

Konge grew up to be a very beautiful young lady. The grandfather always asked her to go with him to many places always showing her off as his '*wife*'. No one ever suspected any mischief to be brewing since this is the accepted norm of that culture.

With time he took the joke a bit further by always touching her inappropriately despite her resistance. Her grandmother was unfriendly to her and always treated her he as a co-wife. Konge could never breath a word about this to her. She was not close to her parents. Who was there for her to confide in? Who could believe her?

Finally, the grandfather raped her. The grandmother got to know about it and became an even greater enemy to this teenage '*co-wife*'.

Her grandmother bewitched her. She dedicated her to a demon which would serve as a husband to her so that she left the grandfather alone. It is not uncommon for women to bewitch their co-wives by dedicating them to incubus; a spirit husband (more about this topic in my book "***Spiritual Female Problems***"). I have prayed for some men who were bewitched by their male competitors by dedicating them to a spirit wife; succubus.

Konge's life changed for the worse. A spirit always raped her during the nights. There she was, home became a crucible. The grandmother ensured it was not a dream come true for her but a living nightmare. She was traumatized. With time she grew so weary with the persecution and eloped with a young man in a desperate attempt to try and find some relief.

Konge was away from her grandmother's territory but incubus remained an invisible enemy who still raped her during the nights.

Whenever she went to bed, she would see a man coming towards her. She would feel so paralyzed, unable to shout for help or even lift a finger. She could not call on the Name of Jesus. At times this spirit would strangle her causing her to gasp for breath. She developed so many strange diseases which the hospitals didn't seem to have any answer for. She became frigid. The bed of roses she expected her new home to be was now full of *'thorns'*. She and her boyfriend became so poor. They felt like a very thick blanket of poverty was looming over their heads all the time. Every business they invested in simply caused them sorrow instead of joy. Unreasonable legal and medical emergencies calling for big expenditures became common place in their lives. It was as if there was an invisible budget drawn by satan to which their money always went.

After a series of deliverance services, Konge became free. The diseases disappeared. She and her boyfriend got married in Church. They began to prosper. It is so hard for a child of God to prosper and be in health unless there are living a life free of demonic oppression. It is also hard to keep your deliverance unless you are willing to live a holy life. It is written in Obadiah 1:17, *"But upon mount Zion shall be deliverance, and there shall be holiness; and the house of Jacob shall possess their possessions".* Deliverance empowers you to live a holy life. A holy life empowers you to enjoy the blessings of God. Therefore; deliverance, then holiness, and finally possession.

2.   Dedicated to an ostrich.

A young man came to our Church in Uganda. He was born in a polygamous family where witchcraft was the trend of the day. In such families some women bewitch their co-wives and their step children so as to keep them in bondage while they themselves accumulate wealth. They also do their best spiritually to win the heart of their husband. In the same way, they seek for help from witches in a desperate attempt to protect themselves and their children.

This young man's mother consulted a witch and had him initiated into witchcraft at an early stage of his life so as to have him supposedly protected. Animal blood sacrifices were made, several rituals were performed, demons were invoked, his body was tattooed, et cetera. From that point onwards, he became a habitation of demons. The witch told her that he would always be *"protected by the power of an ostrich"*. That is how his young brothers and sisters were to be protected as well so that no step mother would ever bewitch them.

Encouraged that some help was promised, they returned home to a false sense of security.

Poverty and sickness were a mark of their family. Whenever this young man or his brothers expected some good news perhaps for a good job or a good financial deal, they would dream of an ostrich. That always marked the end of the deal.

His life was marked by recurring of evil cycles of defeat. Those retrogressive ostrich dreams haunted his life. He was exasperated but this was a family secret he had pledged to tell no one.

I got a word of knowledge about his situation so I called him out for deliverance during our Sunday morning service. He renounced those evil blood covenants he had been initiated into. That power of demonic bondage was broken. He was set free from demonic oppression. A few days after that, he was employed by the government. His life made a very quick U-turn for the better. His brothers too began to prosper.

There are so many people who struggle with problems which began during the early stages of their lives.

Chapter

5.

She lost seven husbands

23.   Jesus said unto him, If thou canst believe, all things are possible to him that believeth.

23.   The same day came to Him the Sadducees, which say that there is no resurrection, and asked him,

24.   saying, Master, Moses said,
If a man die, having no children,
his brother shall marry his wife,
and raise up seed unto his
brother.

25.   Now there were with us
seven brethren: and the first, when
he had married a wife, deceased,
and, having no issue, left his wife
unto his brother:

26.   likewise the second also,
and the third, unto the seventh.

27.   And last of all the woman
died also.

28.   Therefore in the resurrection
whose wife shall she be of the
seven? for they all had her.

29. Jesus answered and said unto them, Ye do err, not knowing the scriptures, nor the power of God.

- Matthew 22:23-29.

The old saying still rings a bell. *"The Pharisees believed in the resurrection. The Sadducees believed not in the resurrection. That's why they're sad you see!"*

They were obviously talking about an eternity they did not believe in. Isn't it very interesting that people who doubt miracles spend so much time discussing them and many atheists think about God more times than they think about His non-existence?

The Lord Jesus gave them a very good answer. Their major problem hinged upon their ignorance of God's Word and His power.

"Ye do err, not knowing the scriptures, nor the power of God".

Ignorance of God's Word and of His power is the greatest cause of problems in the body of Christ today.

These men were very religious. They observed the life of this woman as she suffered calamity after calamity. They took note of her problems but had no power to deliver her from her from the monster who killed her husbands all the time. What a traumatic life she lived!

Religion identifies problems, sets rules by which one's life should be governed but has no answer for that person's spiritual challenges. Some religious people go through life oppressed by demons simply because they do not know *"the scriptures, nor the power of God"*.

Religion is the quest of humanity for the invisible eternal God. Salvation is when we allow God to find us. God is omniscient, omnipresent and omnipotent well as we have so many limitations. It is so much easier when we allow Him to find us by surrendering to His will as spelt out in the Bible than us trying to find Him.

There was a girl at my high school who had a similar problem. The first boy who expressed interest in her got a very severe excruciating headache and could hardly study. He had been a very bright student but his grades became very low all of a sudden. The second boy who dated her died in a car accident. The third boy who dated her was expelled from school. Later on he committed suicide.

There are so many men and women who cannot stay married however much they try. Whoever they date or get married to gets a very big problem. If they happen to stay married then extreme poverty becomes their portion. Some of the spouses end up in jail or die mysteriously. This problem could be rooted in evil covenants, witchcraft, et cetera.

At times it is with men. Whoever gets married dies prematurely or gets recurring unexplained challenges that curtail his joy.

There is power in the blood of Jesus to set free every captive of sin, devils and disease in Jesus' Name.

Chapter

6.

Jesus the Sacrificial Lamb

The human race was created in the image and likeness of God. God made us for life, love, light, dignity, dominion, immeasurable wealth and so much more.[1] His image meant we were to be as holy as He is. His likeness meant we were to function the same way He functions. We were created to be imitators of God.[2]

---

[1] Genesis 1:27-30.

[2] Ephesians 5:1.

Our ancestors (Adam and Eve) were deceived by satan that if they rebelled against God, they would become as wise as He is and be like Him. They believed that lie and ate fruit of the tree which God had forbidden them.[3] The human race (in Adam) rejected the counsel of God and obeyed the serpent thereby surrendering our God given place of authority to the devil.[4] Since then, the entire human race became acquainted with unrighteousness, stress and sorrow.[5] We became strangers to God's righteousness, peace and joy.[6]

Adam and Eve did not need to try and become like God. They were made in His image. They were to be as holy as He is. They did not need to listen to the serpent concerning what to do. They were made in the likeness of God so they would function like

---

[3] Genesis 2:15-17; 3:1-6.

[4] Genesis 3:1-6, Romans 6:14

[5] Genesis 3:16-19.

[6] Romans 14:17.

Him. For instance, Adam had such wisdom that he named every bird and beast.[7] He literally governed the whole planet and was in charge of every creature before the fall.

Sin has repercussions. The justice of God demanded that sin be punished. The only way we could pay for our sin was by being eternally separated from the love and fellowship of God. What a terrible eternity that would be!

The rebellion of humanity did not take God by surprise. God knew we would let Him down. In His mercy and grace He had a redemptive plan in place. The Lamb was slain long even before any human being ever walked on the face of the earth.[8]

---

[7] Genesis 2:19-20.

[8] Revelation 13:8.

8.   But God commendeth His love toward us, in that while we were yet sinners, Christ died for us

- Romans 5:8.

Even now, there should be no question about the guilty of humanity before the just and holy God. *"For all have sinned, and come short of the glory of God"* – Romans 3:23. I love the next verse; *"Being justified freely by His grace through the redemption that is in Christ Jesus"* – Romans 3:24. What God did for us is much more glorious than what we did against Him.

Jesus Christ, God's only begotten Son, the sinless eternal Word of God was made flesh and dwelt among us. This reminds me about Billy Graham's story of a little ant.

Billy Graham equated our situation to that of a human being who creates a little creature called an ant. Being the creator of the ant, he loves the little ant and takes care of it. One day he sees the ant heading toward death, so what does he do? Is it enough to tell the ant that it was going to die? The problems are overwhelming. One, the ant doesn't think as he thinks. Two, it can't hear him. Three, it can't see its creator. Four, it can't understand him. If he tries to touch it, he may kill it. If he puts his hand in front of it, the ant will climb over his hand and keep going. What can he do? The only thing to do is become an ant and say, 'Don't go that way; you are going to die. Follow me. That is exactly what God did when His Word was mad flesh and dwelt among us. We called His Name Jesus.[9]

In the Old Testament days, animal blood would be shed so as to cover the sins of people. For instance, an adulterer or a thief would have a lamb slain for them so as to escape the repercussions of their sin. However, the blood of animals only covered

---

[9] Matthew 1:18-25

people's sins. Covering a thing does not make it nonexistent. Besides, animals being inferior to humanity could not have blood capable of solving our sin problem. God had a better plan. That plan was the incarnation of Jesus Christ.

He was born into this world as our Sacrificial Lamb who would be slain for our sins.[10] He took our place in the courtroom of God's justice and was condemned so that we would be justified. He was rejected so that we would be accepted.

> 18. For Christ also hath once suffered for sins, **the Just for the unjust**, that He might bring us to God, being put to death in **the** flesh, but quickened by **the** Spirit:
>
> - 1 Peter 3:18.

---

[10] John 1:29

Right now, every sinner who comes to God through Christ is forgiven because of one eternal truth; the Lord Jesus took our place in the *'courtroom'* of God's justice. The sinless One was made sin.[11] He became guilty in our stead. The penalty we should have endured was laid upon Him. He *"was delivered for our offences, and was raised again for our justification"* - Romans 4:25.

21. For He *(the Father)* hath made Him *(Jesus)* to be sin for us, who knew no sin; that we might be made the righteousness of God in Him.

- 2 Corinthians 5:21.

The foundational truth of Christianity is that Christ Jesus died on the cross for our sins[12]. In this way he fulfilled the old covenant

---

[11] 2 Corinthians 5:21.

[12] 1 Corinthians 15:3-4.

sacrificial system, reconciled us to God, and changed our lives forever. We don't have to continue living in sin. We have the right, privilege and obligation of becoming sons and daughters of God. We can and should stand for righteousness.

There was more to the redemption than solving the sin problem and getting us back to God. In the redemption is contained our absolute freedom from every form of oppression by the enemy. The ultimate victory over the bondage of sin, devils and disease was not for the Lord Jesus Christ. He did not need it. He did it all for us.

> 25. And having spoiled principalities and powers, he made a shew of them openly, triumphing over them in it.
>
> - Colossians 2:15.

The Lord Jesus disarmed the principalities and powers. He triumphed over them. The kingdom of darkness is eternally defeated. Whenever the Name of Jesus is mentioned, that victory is displayed.

We are in such a privileged position in a territory where satan and his cohorts have no authority.

> 13. Who hath delivered us from the kingdom of darkness, and hath translated us into the Kingdom of His dear Son.
>
> - Colossians 1:13.

We have been authorized to use the invincible Name of Jesus.[13] He literally gave us the power of attorney to use His Name.[14]

---

[13] Mark 16:17-18.

[14] John 14:14.

Whatever He overcame, we too can overcome in His Name. We are seated together with Him in heavenly places.[15] Whatever belongs to Him is ours in His Name.[16] Him alone is the only true foundation.[17] He is the Rock of ages.[18]

---

[15] Ephesians 2:4-6.

[16] John 16:15; 2 Corinthians 1:20.

[17] 1 Corinthians 3:11.

[18] Psalm 18:31

Chapter

7.

Establishing a godly foundation

God has done for us all that we need to live victoriously. He has given us the authority we need to demolish evil foundations and so that we build upon Christ the Rock of Ages.

10. See, I have this day set thee over the nations and over the kingdoms, to root out, and to pull

down, and to destroy, and to throw down, to build, and to plant.

- Jeremiah 1:10.

We are in such a privileged position that no power in hell can reign over us without our permission *(either knowingly or ignorantly).*

For every structure that serves as a basis for the enemy's attacks against us, we will do as Jeremiah was told:

(1) We will root out;

(2) We will pull down;

(3) We will destroy and

(4) We throw down.

After that:

(1). We will build upon Christ the only sure Foundation – 1 Corinthians 3:11.

(2). We will plant. How shall we plant?

a. By our speech *(a deliberate, perpetual positive confession of what God says about us in His Word – Hebrews 10:23).*

b. By our walk *(Let our lives be modeled after Christ – Colossians 2:6; Hebrews 12:1-3).*

c. By our work *(whatever we do in word or deed, let it be to the glory of God – 1 Corinthians 10:31; Colossians 3:17).*

In this chapter, I would like us to be more practical by going straight into prayer concerning the things we have discussed in our previous chapters. It is not enough to talk about swimming if one never gets down to the swimming pool to practice what they were taught.

However, it is also very important for us to know that the benefits of Calvary are a right of only those who chose to accept Jesus Christ as their Lord and Saviour. By His grace, God works miracles even for the unbelieving but only His children have the unquestionable right to demand and possess the promises in His Word.[1]

Beloved, in case you have never given your life to Jesus Christ to become your Lord and Saviour, I have good news for you. You can become a child of God right now. Allow me to lead you in a prayer of repentance as written below. There is need for you to say this prayer out loudly and clearly from the bottom of your heart:

"Dear Lord God, I acknowledge that I am a sinner, unworthy of your fellowship and promises.

"I know that Your Son, Jesus Christ died for my sins and was raised from the dead for

---

[1] Isaiah 45:11.

my justification. I know that He is in heaven seated on Your right hand.

"Have mercy upon me. Please forgive me.

"I do now receive and confess Your Son Jesus Christ as my Lord and savior.

"Father, thank You. So much for my salvation. In the Name of Jesus Christ. Amen."

If you have decided to commit your life to Christ, it will be important for you to belong to a Bible believing Church whose leaders are subject to the written Word of God. They will teach you the Word of God. They will pray for you to be filled with the Holy Spirit. Now you are a believer.

The inward evidence to the believer of his or her salvation is the direct witness of the Holy Spirit (Romans 8:16). The outward evidence to all people is a life of righteousness and true holiness. This kind of life rejects such behavior as sexual immorality and sexual perversion, lust, incest, idolatry, envy, murder, strife, drunkenness, deceit, malice, gossip, slander, insolence, arrogance, boasting, promoting evil deeds, disobedience, greed, covetousness and all forms of moral depravity (Romans 1:18-32; Colossians 3:5-6).

You will need to bear fruit. *"The fruit of the spirit is love, joy, peace, longsuffering, gentleness, goodness, faith, meekness, temperance: against such there is no law"* (Galatians 5:22-23).

I pray that you will have a wonderful time living a life of obedience to God. In case we do not meet here on earth, we will meet along the golden streets and will forever rejoice in the presence of our Father.

Now you have a right to demolish every evil foundation upon which your life or even bloodline had been based for so many years

Once again allow me to lead you in another prayer. This time it is a prayer to *"root out"*, *"pull down"*, *"destroy"* and to *"throw down"* every evil foundation in your life and family and work. We will also make a declaration to establish a godly foundation, to build, and to plant seeds for the benefit of your spirit, your soul, flesh and bloodline.

The axe should be laid on the root. Our Lord Jesus said by our words we shall be justified.[2] It is also written that with the mouth confession is made unto salvation.[3] Salvation is a compound word which includes the saving of our souls, deliverance, healing, restoration and so much more. Therefore, by our confession, we obtain deliverance.

---

[2] Matthew 12:27.

[3] Romans 10:10.

Confession   precedes   possession. *"Whosoever shall say ... shall have whatsoever he saith"* – Mark 11:23-24.

I wrote a prayer in my book; ***"Break the curses"*** which I believe to be of great importance for this subject as well. We have received numerous testimonies of people who obtained their deliverance while they declared the words of the prayer you are about to read. I have amended it for the purpose of what we need to accomplish here.

Let us pray:

Dear heavenly Father, I come to you in the Name of my Lord and Saviour Jesus Christ!

Thank you for loving me and that you demonstrated Your love by sending Your Son Jesus to pay the supreme price for my redemption. I know that the Lord Jesus was wounded for our transgressions, He was bruised for our iniquities, the chastisement of our peace was upon Him and with His stripes we were healed. I know that the Lord Jesus is the only true eternal foundation upon which my life should be established.

I acknowledge that I am guilty of the sins in my life and in my ancestors' lives which were the basis for evil foundations or which contributed to cracks in the foundation of my life and family. I repent of all those sins in the Name of Jesus Christ.

Father, Your Word says I will not be forgiven if I do not forgive those who have wronged me. Father, please give me the grace to forgive in Jesus' Name. I do now forgive all those people who wronged me causing me sorrow. I forgive you … (mention their names and what they did if you can remember it). I declare myself free from the spirit of un-forgiveness in Jesus' Name!

Father, please forgive me for every sin I have committed due to the lust of the flesh, the lust of the eyes and the pride of life. Please forgive me for every evil and careless word which I have spoken or meditated upon. I cancel all those words and their negative effects upon my life in Jesus' Name. Let the words of my mouth and the meditation of my heart be acceptable in Your sight, O Lord my Strength and my Redeemer in Jesus' Name!

In the Name of Jesus Christ the Son of the Living God, I repent of all sexual perversions including pornography, sexual fantasies, fornication, adultery, homosexuality, lesbianism, masturbation and all forms of moral depravity whether committed by me or any one of my relatives and covenant friends living or dead.

I repent of all acts of rebellion, disobedience, financial sins, sorcery, divination and all sorts of witchcraft and occult involvement. I repent for every idle word which I have spoken or believed in and every oath or pledge for which I am held responsible. I repent for all evil altars raised by my family and I. I declare their sacrifices nullified and those evil altars destroyed in Jesus' Name. Let me be cleansed by the blood of Your Son Jesus Christ.

Father, Your Word declares that when I confess my sins, You are faithful and just to forgive me my sins and to cleanse me from all unrighteousness. Basing on Your Word, I acknowledge Your faithfulness and thank You for forgiving me. I stand forgiven. All my sins are remitted in Jesus' Name!

satan, hear this in Jesus Name. I do not belong to you any longer. I am a child of God, saved by His grace and cleansed from all unrighteousness by the blood of Jesus. You have no legal claim over my life any longer.

In the Name of Jesus, I thank You Father for the whole armour which You have provided for me according to the scriptures. Right now, I fasten my loins with the belt of truth. I stand having on the breast plate of righteousness. My feet are shod with the preparation of the gospel of peace. Above all I take the shield of faith and right now I declare all the fiery darts of the wicked quenched. I take the helmet of salvation and the sword of the Spirit which is the Word of God. Help me pray with all prayer and supplication in the Spirit, and watching thereunto with all perseverance for all saints. I put on Christ as my garment and let no provision be made whatsoever for the flesh to reign over me. I declare all this in the Name of Jesus Christ.

Father, in the Name of Your Son Jesus Christ, I counter all the petitions of satan and his cohorts against me. The blood of Jesus testifies that I am Your righteousness in Christ, and that I am the apple of Your eye. I thank You Father because You disappoint the devices of the crafty so that their hands cannot perform their enterprises against me. Please do not grant the powers of darkness anything they ask of you concerning me. Let all satan's desires concerning my life, family, friends and property be frustrated in Jesus' Name!

In the Name of Jesus Christ, the Son of the Living God, I break every communication which the astrologers, witches, warlocks, and all wicked beings have with celestial creatures against me. Let every satanic enchantment against me be confounded in Jesus' Name!

In Jesus' Name, I declare the blood of Jesus Christ against every evil sacrifice offered to the powers of darkness against me. Let every satanic altar and all high places raised against me be permanently destroyed in Jesus' Name. Let every demonic device against me be destroyed in Jesus Name.

In the Name of Jesus, I cancel every accusation brought up against me! I cancel every judgment against me by the kingdom of darkness and I nullify every verdict against me by the kingdom of darkness, in the Name of Jesus Christ. I command all panels and committees set up against me to be scattered into oblivion in Jesus' Name! Let every evil voice and tongue against me be permanently silenced by the power of God in Jesus' Name!

In the Name of Jesus Christ, the Son of the Living God, I speak to you earth and all earthly beings to reject the voices of witches, warlocks and all wicked beings against me right now. In Jesus' Name I command you water bodies and everything that is in you to reject the voices of witches, warlocks and all wicked beings against me. In the Name of Jesus Christ, the Son of the Living God, I command every spiritual storm and turbulence against me to cease right now.

In the Name of Jesus, I take authority over every work of unrighteousness. In the

Name of Jesus, I renounce every ungodly vow and pledge which I have ever made to satan, to any of his priests, or to anyone living or dead. In Jesus' Name I place under the blood of Jesus, every ungodly pact, agreement, or covenant of which I am part, knowingly or unknowingly, whether it was done by me or anyone living or dead. All those ungodly agreements of which I am part knowingly or unknowingly, whether entered into by the blood of humans, animals, or birds, or by the sap of trees, or any other thing are hereby placed under the blood of Jesus Christ and I declare them permanently broken in the Name of Jesus Christ, the Son of the Living God.

In the Name of Jesus, I take authority over and I break every curse working in my life, or in the lives of any of my family members. I break all curses of failure, poverty, lack, indebtedness, endless financial frustrations, sicknesses and diseases, witchcraft, premature death, vagabond, rejection, abuse, rape, frigidity and family destruction. In the Name of Jesus Christ, I break all curses working against my marriage and children. Let every garment and programme of premature death imposed upon me be destroyed in Jesus' Name!

In the Name of Jesus Christ, I destroy every yoke of bondage linked to my birth day and my birth place. In the Name of Jesus, I break myself loose from every evil foundation affecting my life in any way known or unknown to me. I break every hex, jinx, spell, and every negative words spoken over my life and over the lives of all those near and dear to me!

In the Name of Jesus, I defy all the barriers set for me by satan and every ungodly being living or dead. I break every spirit of caging, every fetter, chain, shackle, cord, habit, and evil cycle over my life in Jesus' Name.

I thank You Father that I was redeemed from the curse of the law when my Lord and

Saviour Jesus Christ was hanged on the cross at Calvary. Thank You for the blood of Jesus by which my sins are remitted and by which all curses affecting my life have lost their ground.

I thank You Father that I am the temple of God and that the Holy Spirit resides in me. I rejoice in Your truth that I am the apple of Your eye. The power and influence of the devourer is broken over my life. Abraham's blessings are mine. No weapon that is formed against me shall prosper and every evil tongue that rises up against me in judgment shall be permanently defeated in Jesus' Name. I am more than a conqueror through You Who loved me. I am the head and not the tail. I shall not die but live to declare the works of the Lord in Jesus' Name!

Father, in Jesus' Name I thank You because Your divine power has given me all things that pertain unto life and godliness. I have been blessed with all spiritual blessings in heavenly places in Christ. I thank You

Father because You supply all my need according to Your riches in glory by Christ Jesus. I bless Your holy Name because You load me with benefits every day.

Father, I agree with you and in Jesus' Name I declare; my Lord Jesus was wounded for my transgressions, He was bruised for my iniquities, the chastisement of my peace was upon Him and with His stripes I was healed. In Jesus' Name I declare that I have the mind of Christ and I am like a tree that is planted by the streams of water, which yields its fruits in season and whose leaves do not wither. Whatever I do shall prosper because the blessing of God rests upon my life and every work of my hands in Jesus' Name!

In the Name of Jesus Christ the Son of the Living God, I resist you satan. Flee from my life in Jesus Name!

I command all spirits of sexual perversions, self-pity double mindedness, unbelief, caging, evil control of my life, fear, divorce, rejection, ugliness, bondages of all kinds, rage, rape, abuse of every kind, strife, contention, frigidity, impotence, separation, fibroids, cancer, sexual perversions, unnecessary pains during the menstruation periods, widowhood, single-parenthood, spinsterhood, anxiety, despair, sadism, masochism and every other evil spirit mentioned or unmentioned to come out of me in the Name of Jesus Christ!

Let every power passing evil currents into my life be bound in Jesus' Name! I command you evil currents against my life, desist from your maneuvers and operations against me right now in Jesus' Name. Let every attack against me through dreams be frustrated in Jesus' Name! Let every power arrayed against me in the high places, on land, in the waters, in the jungles, or under the earth be bound and broken in Name of Jesus Christ. Let my name be blotted out of every evil register and out of all satanic records in Jesus' Name. Let every doorway used by the enemy against me be closed right now in Jesus' Name. I break every system of communication used by the powers of darkness against me in Jesus' Name!

In the Name of Jesus the Son of the Living God I declare civil strife and great confusion in the camp of every principality, power, rulers of darkness of this world and wicked spirits in high places which operate against me. In the Name of Jesus, I tread upon all serpents, scorpions and every power of the enemy, and I declare that nothing shall by any means hurt me.

I declare today that I am a child of God, purchased by the blood of the Lamb. Lord, I thank You for my salvation, deliverance and healing in the Name of Jesus' Christ!

═══════════════════

It is important to note that some demons are stubborn and may require an anointed, experienced deliverance minister to help you even after the prayer you just said. One thing remains true, all their covenants are broken, and every legal claim satan had over your life is null and void. The evil foundation is demolished. Your life is now founded upon Jesus Christ the Rock of Ages. You are free in Jesus' Name. Hallelujah for the blood of Jesus Christ, the Lamb of God!

Chapter

8.

How to maintain your deliverance.

I have almost transferred this chapter verbatim from the seventh chapter of my book; *"Spiritual Female Problems"* because the truths contained therein serve the same purpose as in this case. There is no other scriptural way of maintaining one's deliverance known to me contrary to what we have here. So, why reinvent the wheel?

It is very painful for a person to be touched by the power of God only to return to their bondage a few moments later. The truth that a demon has been cast out of a person is no guarantee that satan has lost interest in that person. The Lord Jesus taught us that evil spirits are desperate for flesh and blood. They always try to do anything within their limited ability to repossess any house they may have been thrown out of!

43. When the unclean spirit is gone out of a man, he walketh through dry places, seeking rest, and findeth none.

44. Then he saith, i will return into my house from whence i came out; and when he is come, he findeth *it* empty, swept, and garnished.

45.   Then goeth he, and taketh
with himself seven other spirits
more wicked than himself, and they
enter in and dwell there: and the
last *state* of that man is worse than
the first.   Even so shall it be also
unto this wicked generation.

-        Matthew 12:43-45.

There is need for you to establish a firewall so
no power of darkness can ever have access
to your life again.   I have discovered some
twelve keys in God's Word that will help you
keep your deliverance.

1.   Salvation

The first and most important key to enjoying
any blessing from God is Salvation.   You
cannot have access to God's covenant
blessings until you surrender to Jesus to be
your Lord and Saviour!   There cannot be any

other better foundation for your life and plans except Christ.[1]

Anyone good or evil can obtain a miracle from God.[2] However, the power to keep a miracle is a reserve of only those who are in a covenant relationship with God; His children saved by the grace.

The promises of God are conditional. They always bear an "IF".[3] We need to be born into the family of God so we may have the right to His promises.

The Kingdom of God is righteousness, peace, and joy in the Holy Ghost.[4] Except a person

---

[1] 1 Corinthians 3:11.

[2] Matthew 5:44-45.

[3] 2 Chronicles 7:14.

[4] Romans 14:17.

be born again, he or she cannot see *(perceive, experience, enjoy and take possession of the promises of)* the Kingdom of God.[5]

2.   God's Word

It is very important to have a Bible of your own and to study it regularly. The enemy of your soul, satan is not scared of your words or talents. Satan is defeated by the Word of the Living God. We are encouraged to soak ourselves into God's Word and let it be part of our lives.

> 8.   This book of the law shall not depart out of thy mouth; but thou shalt meditate therein day and night, that thou mayest observe to do according to all that is written

---

[5] John 3:3.

therein: for then thou shalt make thy way prosperous, and then thou shalt have good success..

- Joshua 1:8.

Good success has its roots in the Word of God. That is one of the reasons we should spend time studying God's Word.

16. Let the word of Christ dwell in you richly in all wisdom; teaching and admonishing one another in psalms and hymns and spiritual songs, singing with grace in your hearts to the Lord.

- Colossians 3:16.

The Word of God is our bread.[6] A starved body cannot grow. Just like our physical bodies need to be fed and nourished, we

---

[6] Deuteronomy 8:3, John 6:31-35.

need to feed on this heavenly bread so we may grow spiritually and be victorious in life.

3. Church

It is important to find a Bible believing, Bible practising congregation and be part of it. They will baptize you by immersion into water and pray for you to be filled with the Holy Spirit. They will teach the principles of God to you as revealed in His Word.

God's Word encourages us not to be churchless. It is the privilege and obligation of every child of God to belong to a God glorifying church. There are quite a number of things you will only overcome when you join yourself to people who love and obey God.

God has established divine leadership in the church.[7] You will grow and be victorious with

---

[7] Ephesians 4:11-14.

their Bible based counsel and spiritual covering.

> 25.   Not forsaking the assembling of ourselves together, as the manner of some *is*; but exhorting *one another*. and so much the more, as ye see the day approaching.
>
> - Hebrews 10:25.

4.   Prayer

Prayer builds your fellowship with God.   It is easier for a prayerful Christian to exercise the power of God than a prayerless one.   God empowers those who wait upon Him in prayer.[8]   There are challenges and temptations which never come your way just

---

[8] Isaiah 40:29-31.

because you prayed.[9] We are encouraged to pray without ceasing.

17.   Pray without ceasing.

-    1 Thessalonians 5:17.

-

We should pray with all prayer and supplication in the Spirit.[10] Whenever we pray we drink the presence of God in. His presence hovers upon those who wait upon Him in prayer.

Once we are filled with the Holy Ghost and we continue praying in tongues we build ourselves up on our most holy faith.[11] We should pray with our understanding and in tongues.

---

[9] Matthew 26:41; Mark 14:38.

[10] Ephesians 6:18.

[11] Jude 20.

14. For if I pray in an *unknown* tongue, my spirit prayeth, but my understanding is unfruitful.

- 1 Corinthians 14:14.

Prayerlessness is a kind of pride against the Person of God. A prayerless person lives their life as though they have all the wisdom and power to deal with life's issues and so do not need God's grace. Prayerless people are an easy prey for the devil.

Prayerlessness also makes a person beastlike and causes the wrath of God to come upon that person's life.[12]

5. The Blood of Jesus

There is awesome power in the blood of Jesus. In the Old Testament Job used to

---

[12] Jeremiah 10:20-25.

keep his family safe from every attack of satan by shedding the blood of animals. A hedge of protection was established around his family which satan could not easily break through was it not for Job's fears.

On one occasion God challenged satan about Job's life and satan outlined five things which discouraged him as far as Job's life was concerned. In Job 1:10 there is a point after every punctuation mark.

> 10. Hast not thou made an hedge about him, and about his house, and about all that he hath on every side? thou hast blessed the work of his hands, and his substance is increased in the land.
>
> - Job 1:10.

Whenever Job shed the blood of animals:

a. A hedge of protection was established around him.

b.　A hedge of protection was established around his household (family).

c.　A hedge of protection was established around his investments and resources on every side.

d.　There was a blessing which came upon the work of his hands.

e.　His substance would be increased in the land.

If the blood of animals did so much for an Old Testament servant of God, how much more shall the blood of Christ do for God's children? Every time we declare the blood of Jesus Christ, the attacks of satan are thwarted (I encourage you to get my book; *"The Blood That Speaketh Better Things"*).

6.　Close every satanic inlet

It is very important for you to identify the areas where you have been delivered and every doorway which the powers of darkness used to enter into your life. Make a quality decision to close them permanently. For example, if someone lonely used to be a prostitute it may not be the best decision for that person to be the sole counsellor of a lonely lecher in a dark solitary place.

satan is crafty and quite persistent. Once you allow him a place in your life, he will take advantage of it to your destruction. Close every doorway and do not allow him to recapture any of those areas in your life where he has been defeated.

43. When the unclean spirit is gone out of a man, he walketh through dry places, seeking rest, and findeth none.

44. Then he saith, I will return into my house from whence I came out; and when he is come, he

findeth *it* empty,   swept,   and garnished.

45.   Then goeth he, and taketh with himself seven other spirits more wicked than himself, and they enter in and dwell there: and the last *state* of that man is worse than the first. Even so shall it be also unto this wicked generation.

- Matthew 12:43-45.

Go and sin no more lest that which is worse comes upon you![13]

7.   Apply the mind of Christ

As a child of God, your mind should be renewed by the Word of God on a regular

---

[13] John 5:14.

basis so that you may not be enslaved to any unholy thoughts bred in hell.[14]

> 8. Finally, brethren, whatsoever things are true, whatsoever things *are* honest, whatsoever things *are* just, whatsoever things *are* pure, whatsoever things *are* lovely, whatsoever things *are* of good report; if *there be* any virtue, and if *there be* any praise, think on these things.
>
> - Philippians 4:8.

One of the quickest means of becoming an enemy of God is to have a carnal mind.[15] We have the mind of Christ.[16] God has given us the Spirit of power, love and a sensible, sober,

---

[14] Romans 12:2; James 1:21.

[15] Romans 8:6-8.

[16] 1 Corinthians 2:16

sound mind.[17] We should exercise it all the time. Let the words of our mouths and the meditations of our hearts be acceptable to God.[18]

When your mind is renewed, you become a candidate of God's blessings and true prosperity.[19] There is need to bring into captivity every thought to the obedience of Christ.[20]

8.   Remain sober and vigilant

There will be need for you to be sober and vigilant all the time.[21] This becomes very easy if you dress up in the whole armour of God all

---

[17] 2 Timothy 1:7

[18] Psalms 19:14.

[19] Psalms 1:1-3; 3 John 2

[20] 2 Corinthians 10:5.

[21] 1 Peter 5:8.

the time.[22] The armour of God builds a very strong firewall around you so that no demon can touch you.

God has given us authority to deny satan a place in our lives. So, neither give place to the devil.[23]

> 8. Be sober, be vigilant; because your adversary the devil, as a roaring lion, walketh about, seeking whom he may devour:
>
> - 1 Peter 5:8.

9. Rebuke satan as a person

The Lord Jesus rebuked satan and demons on a number of occasions.[24] satan is not an

---

[22] Ephesians 6:10-18

[23] Ephesians 4:27.

[24] Matthew 16:23; 17:18.

idea. satan is a person. he is an eternally defeated foe.[25] In the midst of His temptations the Lord Jesus spoke God's Word to satan and satan's schemes failed.[26] That is what a child of God should do.

Whenever any temptation comes your way trying to drag you into your sinful past, remember it is satan's snare so he can have access to your life once again. Learn to say out loudly and clearly: *"satan, I resist you in the Name of Jesus Christ".* When you resist the devil, he will flee from you.[27]

> 9. Whom resist stedfast in the faith, knowing that the same afflictions are accomplished in your brethren that are in the world.
>
> - 1 Peter 5:9.

---

[25] 1 Corinthians 2:6-8; Colossians 2:15; Hebrews 2:14.

[26] Matthew 4:3-11.

[27] James 4:7.

Do not allow those old habits to take advantage of you again. Do not allow sin to be your Lord any longer.[28]

10. Agree with people of like faith in prayer

18. Verily I say unto you, Whatsoever ye shall bind on earth shall be bound in heaven: and whatsoever ye shall loose on earth shall be loosed in heaven.

19. Again I say unto you, That if two of you shall agree on earth as touching any thing that they shall ask, it shall be done for them of my Father which is in heaven.

---

[28] Romans 6:14.

20. For where two or three are gathered together in my name, there am I in the midst of them.

- Matthew 18:18-20.

You can always bind the demons on assignment against you, on a daily basis. You have authority to loose the angels of God to minister to you[29] and to defeat every evil spirit against you.

The Lord Jesus said He could have asked the Father for twelve legions of angels when attacked.[30] God is no respecter of persons.[31] Whatever He could do for Jesus, He desires to do for us because He loves us just like He loves Christ.[32]

---

[29] Hebrews 1:14.

[30] Matthew 26:53.

[31] Acts 10:34.

[32] John 17:22-23.

11. Take your place in Christ and reign with Him

Ignorance limits a person so they cannot fully enjoy what is rightfully theirs. There is need for you to know who you are in Christ and what fully belongs to you because of the finished work of Christ at Calvary.

Remember to learn those verses in the New Testament, especially in the epistles which reveal to you who you are in Christ and what belongs to you because of Calvary. Those which bear phrases such as; "in Whom", "through Him", "in Christ", "in Him". There is great wisdom in learning them by heart and declaring them in season and out of season.[33]

Whatever a believer declares is established.[34] You can change your environment and reign over sin, devils, and diseases by the words you speak.[35]

---

[33] 2 Timothy 4:2.

[34] Job 22:28; Mark 11:23.

[35] Proverbs 18:21.

12. Do the work of an evangelist

One does not have to be an evangelist to preach the gospel. We have all been called to do the work of an evangelist. That is one of the easiest ways for you to make full proof of whatever calling and ministry God has entrusted you with.[36]

When a person proclaims the gospel, they are exercising their God given authority over satan. It is part of our spiritual warfare as children of God.[37]

Proclaiming the good news means you will have to testify about Christ. Whenever you testify about Christ here on earth, He too testifies about you before the Father and before the holy angels of God.[38]

---

[36] 2 Timothy 4:5.

[37] Ephesians 6:15.

[38] Matthew 10:32-33; Luke 12:8-9.

When you testify about the resurrection of Christ, great grace comes upon you.[39]

There are numerous blessings which come upon your life just because you have proclaimed the gospel.[40]

——————————————————

Beloved in Christ, in case this book has been a blessing to you, please write a good review about it on www.amazon.com so that others may be encouraged to read it as well.

Remain blest I Jesus' mighty Name.

---

[39] Acts 4:33.

[40] Isaiah 52:7.

Other books by Moses Nsubuga Sekatawa:

1. Spiritual Female Problems.
2. Have Some Money.
3. Now Faith Is
4. Worshipping God with our resources.
5. Break the curses.
6. The Blood that speaketh better things.

Moses Nsubuga Sekatawa's books are sold on www.amazon.com and many other channels.

1

1

Made in the USA
Middletown, DE
30 July 2020

14050929R00083